EMERGING
VOICES

# 900 Miles from Home

## Ian Crawford

CCBar and piano

DIFFICULTY LEVEL ● ● ●

OXFORD

# 900 Miles from Home

Trad. American
arr. IAN CRAWFORD

Duration: 2.5 mins

Printed in Great Britain

OXFORD UNIVERSITY PRESS, MUSIC DEPARTMENT, GREAT CLARENDON STREET, OXFORD OX2 6DP

walk - in' down the track, I got tears in my eyes, 'cause I'm tryin' to read a

walk - in' down the track, I got tears in my eyes, 'cause I'm tryin' to read a

**BARITONE**

'Cause I'm tryin' to read a

let - ter from my home. If this train runs me right I'll be

let - ter from my home. If this train runs me right I'll be

let - ter from my home. If this train runs me right I'll be

Well, this train I'm rid-in' on is a thou-sand coach-es

Well, this train I'm rid-in' on, yes, a

Thou - sand

long, you can hear her from a mil-lion miles a - way.

thou-sand, you can hear her from a mil-lion miles a - way.

coach - es, you can hear her from a mil-lion miles a - way.

an' I hate to hear that lone-some whis-tle blow._

an' I hate to hear that lone-some whis-tle blow._    I will

an' I hate...    I will

pawn you my wa - gon, I will pawn you my team.

pawn you my wa - gon, I will pawn you my team.

* If the B and A are too low, Baritones may sing the small notes, doubling the Cambiata 2 part.

miles from my home_____ an' I hate...

miles from my home_____ an' I hate to hear that lone-some whis-tle blow.\_

miles from my home_____ an' I hate to hear that lone-some whis-tle blow.\_

I am walk-in' down the track, I got tears in my

I am walk-in' down the track, I got

I got

Music originated by Andrew Jones

ISBN 978-0-19-356192-2